WINCHESTER SCHOOL OF MISSION

05206

D1346390

An Anglo-Saxon
Passion

David Scott is Rector of St Lawrence and St Swithun,
Winchester, and Warden of the Diocesan School of Spirituality.
His *Selected Poems* are published by Bloodaxe Books,
and his first book for SPCK, *Moments of Prayer,*
was published in 1997.

AN ANGLO-SAXON
PASSION

David Scott

First published in Great Britain in 1999
Society for Promoting Christian Knowledge
Holy Trinity Church
Marylebone Road
London NW1 4DU

Copyright © David Scott 1999

All rights reserved. No part of this book may be reproduced or transmitted in
any form or by any means, electronic or mechanical, including
photocopying, recording, or by any information storage and
retrieval system, without permission in writing from the publisher.

Bible quotations are from The Revised English Bible © 1989 Oxford and
Cambridge University Presses, except for extracts from the
Song of Solomon, which are from the Authorized Version of the Bible,
which is the property of the Crown in perpetuity.
Lines from e. e. cummings's poem 'I thank you God for most this
amazing day', from *Selected Poems 1923–1958* (Faber 1972), are
reprinted by permission of Faber and Faber Ltd. Lines from 'The Tree'
by R. S. Thomas, from *Later Poems* (Macmillan 1984), are reprinted
by permission of Macmillan Publishers Ltd.

British Library Cataloguing-in-Publication Data

A catalogue record for this book is available from the British Library

ISBN 0-281-05212-3

Typeset by Pioneer Associates, Perthshire
Printed in Malta by Interprint Ltd

Contents

The Crosse is but a little word;
    but of great contents.
        Bp Lancelot Andrewes

how should tasting touching hearing seeing
breathing any – lifted from the no
of all nothing – human merely being
doubt unimaginable You?
now the ears of my ears awake
and now the eyes of my eyes are opened
                        e. e. cummings

and they shall look upon me whom
    they have pierced
            Zechariah 12.10

Introduction

AD 900. *The second day of the week leading up to the great Paschal Feast. Yesterday was Palm Sunday. We held our palms high, and sang 'Blessed is He who comes in the name of the Lord'. A small plot of land surrounded by the fast flowing waters of the river. The mill race is going frantic with the churning spume. The spring flowers are enjoying the early sun but cautious of the cold. It is cold and damp at dawn and dusk, when I get out of bed and go back to bed, and in the middle of the night when we get up and process to the church to say the night prayers. This week has a bitter sweetness, the pain and the glory, the re-enactment of the last days and hours of Jesus' life. In the church, the great cross which towers above the central altar, the altar of the cross, has been lowered in readiness for veneration, to be gazed at, touched, kissed, knelt by, and decorated, by our community . . .*

. . . a week of fast days, until we cry 'Christ is risen' . . . and such a mixture of feelings. I want just to sit at the feet of Jesus, like Mary of Bethany, and absorb the emotion of it all, and not to have to think too much, or talk too much, or be responsible and organizing, and no doubt that means that a lot of others have to

work harder to let me do my dreaming. To go in my mind the way of the cross, to put on the mind of Christ, as he went on the way of the cross.

So I imagine a nun musing, as she copies 24 prayers from one document onto the 41 leaves of stout vellum, in the weeks leading up to Easter, in the year AD 900. These copied prayers, translated from Latin into English, are what we now have in this book. Who originally wrote the prayers, and under what circumstances, and the circumstances of their copying and use in AD 900, are questions that this introduction hopes to go some way to answering. What holds them all together, author, copier, user, discoverer, translator, meditator, and the prayers themselves, is their subject: the figure of Christ going by way of the cross, through to glory. This is a way that Christians, down the centuries, have desired to, and found ways to, follow. The scribing nun keeps popping up in the introduction. I have assumed her presence and given her words in order to root all the research and the history in the human soul, and to help us remember that prayers are nothing until they find the one who prays.

The prayers collected here are both timeless, and yet they are also placed in time. The more I ponder their timeless quality, the closer I enter into the mystery that is Christ, and to an understanding of my own need of forgiveness. The more I research the likely period in history when they were written, the wider and vaster the horizon becomes. The subjects of the prayers are the last days of Jesus' earthly life, his passion, and resurrection.

Factually, they tell us no more than the Gospels do, but the mind and heart of the writer have very much their own focus. It is possible to read and value these prayers without any historical knowledge at all. Prayers, being about the eternal nature of God's love, are timeless, but let me begin and open a way into them, through my own discovery of them, which was serendipitous.

SEVENTEENTH CENTURY

Written prayers were taking up my interest, and I was reading through the seventeenth-century collection of prayers attributed to Lancelot Andrewes (1559–1626). Prayers are not easily owned, they are gathered. They often come to us anonymously in the liturgy, and are anyone's and everyone's property, whoever finds them useful in their conversation with God is welcome to them. Andrewes' collection, known as the *Private Prayers*, although gathered in the 1600s, contains prayers from all periods of the Christian Church, and through Old Testament texts, especially the Psalms, they bring us the great Hebrew tradition as well. One particular prayer caught my eye:

> Thou who didst will thy glorious head should be
> wounded,
> by it forgive
> what sin soever I have wrought by the senses of
> my head.

Thou who didst will thy sacred hands should be digged,
    by them forgive
        what sin soever I have wrought by unlawful touch,
        unlawful operation.

Thou who didst will thy precious side should be bored
        through,
    by it forgive
        what sin soever I have wrought by unlawful thoughts
        in the heat of lust.

Thou who didst will thy blessed feet should be fastened,
    by them forgive
        what sin soever I have wrought by the going of feet
        swift to evil.

Thou who didst will thy whole body should be distent,
    by it forgive
        what sin soever I have evilly wrought by the means
        of all my members.

(Lancelot Andrewes, *Private Prayers*, tr. F. E. Brightman, 1903 p. 218)

It was the physicality of the prayers that first struck me, and on deeper reflection, it was also the interaction of the physical and the spiritual. It seemed that head, hands, feet, side, and then the whole body, were all in some way still effective, through the experience of Christ's suffering, for our own destiny, and also in some sort of solidarity with my own body. The combination of the physical and the spiritual was a fascinating and powerful mix. It was something I had been struggling with, or concerned about, almost since I was able to know that I could feel. To extend that interest into the world of devotional literature set off a fascinating journey, always with the cross of Christ at its axis, and its effectiveness spreading out into the whole of my life.

A Sixteenth-Century *Book of Hours*

F. E. Brightman (1856–1932), the great liturgical scholar and editor of Andrewes' *Private Prayers*, locates the prayer in a *Book of Hours*, a medieval prayer book of 1514, now kept in the Cambridge University Library. What better excuse to have a week in Cambridge than to spend time hunting up the actual prayer in its original state. And so I found a room near enough to fall out of bed into the University Library, and from there spent a happy week browsing, copying and taking notes.

Horae, or *The Hours*, as the book is called, was full of prayers which Andrewes had incorporated into his *Private Prayers*. It was fascinating to see a pre-Reformation prayer book with so many brutal scratchings out, and sometimes whole prayers cut out which referred to the Virgin Mary, or the particular efficacy of some saint or other. I had learnt about the Reformation in history lessons but here was actual evidence of that ruthless and comprehensive expunging of 'catholic' devotional practice. We often see the scars of this period on the walls of our cathedrals and churches, in the empty niches and jagged edges of stone-work, but here it was in the books.

The medieval prayer was more elaborate than the seventeenth-century one of Andrewes. Andrewes' version is spare and omits references to Mary and angels. The medieval version runs like this:

> Lord Jesus Christ who willed that your glorious head, ven-erated by angels and men, should receive a crown of thorns, so that blood flowed for the redemption of the world, on account of your holy name; and by the merits of the intercession of your blessed mother and all your saints, forgive those sins which I have wrought by the senses of my head: Lord have mercy on me sinner that I am. Amen.

The sense of Jesus 'willing' the passion is the same in both the seventeenth-century prayer and in the medieval prayer, but the sense of penitence is more pronounced in the medieval prayer, and the actual words 'crown of thorns' are used.

The Hours consisted, essentially, of the additional offices, which from the ninth century onwards became the customary supplement to the services of the Canonical Hours, for example, the Offices of the Blessed Virgin Mary and of the Litany, and the Penitential and the Gradual Psalms. One of the great scholars of this material was Edmund Bishop (1846–1917), liturgist and historian, and so I thought I would look his name up in the card index of our local clergy library, to see what he had to say about this sort of passion prayer. Indeed there was a book by Edmund Bishop, called *Liturgia Historica* (Oxford 1918). It contains a series of essays, one of which, 'About an Old Prayer Book', had me glued to the seat with excitement. The magic word was 'Winchester', and there followed a brief but tantalizing reference to the use of this type of prayer in the Anglo-Saxon nunnery of Nunnaminster, in about AD 900. This took me back 600 years from my medieval book, and the Nunnaminster happened to be just across the way from our rectory. The grounds of the nunnery are still there, now a public park, and there is a site recently excavated which has revealed some foundations of the minster church and some stone coffins. To think that these prayers which had been handed on through the centuries might have had their beginning in a community of women, whose grounds and whose spirits are so close to me, just across the way, was almost more excitement than I could contain. But that essay was just to be the beginning of a new and even more enticing chapter in the search for the author of these prayers.

Taking each letter and copying it, correctly I hope, and every now and then spending a bit longer on one letter, the 'A' of approaching at the beginning of St Luke's passion narrative: 'the festival of Unleavened Bread, known as Passover, was Approaching'. It is approaching. It is only a few days away, and I have got to try and get this finished, but the more I rush, the more mistakes I make. I look up now and then and see the top of St Giles' Hill, and the grey skies of this holy week of passion thoughts. There is a tuft of trees on the top of the hill. All hills are Calvary this week, and all trees, crosses. I'm changing a few of the words of the prayers, but haven't told anyone. I have decided to be a 'peccatrix', a woman sinner, not a man sinner. My sense of failure before God this week is very much bound up with me being me. You know that, God. We've talked about it.

A Ninth-Century Anglo-Saxon Manuscript

It was through the Edmund Bishop essay that I read about another book that would bring me even closer to the source of the prayers that had so fascinated me in the Lancelot Andrewes collection. This was an edition of a particular eighth-century manuscript called the *Nunnaminster Manuscript*. Because Nunnaminster was a Winchester foundation, the Hampshire Record Society had published an edition of this manuscript, edited by W. de Gray Birch, in 1889. So far as I know there has been no comprehensive translation of the Latin prayers that are contained within it, and there it was, on the shelves of the County Record Office. I wondered if anyone had looked at it since it was first put there. Being a reference book, there was no chance of taking it out to work on a translation of the prayers, and being pre-twentieth century it could not be photocopied. So I began the laborious process of copying the whole 40 prayers by hand, and at the end of half an hour had succeeded in transcribing three of them. This was obviously going to be a long and frustrating process, not having much time or opportunity to spend in the Record Office.

A day or so later, a retired clergyman let me know that since he was going into sheltered accommodation, he was pruning his library and would I like to come and choose some books. I went to the house, now stripped of most of its books and furniture, except for two piles of books on the bare floor. These he said are for you to choose from and these are for the library. I chose from my pile and was very grateful, and then turning to go, chanced to see that the top book on the other, library pile was Birch's edition of the Nunnaminster prayers titled *An Ancient Manuscript*. Here was the very book that I couldn't borrow from the Record Office, and so desperately wanted. Taking my courage in both hands I asked him if I could have that particular book, since I was hoping to translate the prayers in it. He readily agreed. I had my own copy of the Latin prayers and could now spend as long as I wanted poring over the intricacies of translation. If I didn't believe in providence before that, then I most certainly believed in it afterwards.

AN ANCIENT MANUSCRIPT

It is surprising how a keen interest in a subject can transform a little learning into great use. My Latin is schoolboy Latin, but in translating the prayers I did get a great deal of help from a friend, Peter Cramer, who teaches history at Winchester College.

My translator accomplice was surprised at the prayers, their strangeness. It was no surprise to me, because the Latin was strange enough to start with, but in translation I began to see what he meant. Used to the comparative simplicity of the Prayer Book collects, here were longer prayers, here was the 'I' form as opposed to the more objective 'we' form of the collects, and there was an imagination at work which broke the safe boundaries of the Roman Sacramentaries, from which most of our Prayer Book collects have come.

Conclusions, or suppositions, about the origin of the prayers took second place to the sheer hard work of the translation. I began to notice repeated phrases, and a common structure to the prayers: they began with an address to God, and then an aspect of Christ's passion was isolated, such as the ear of Christ or the nose or the side, and the suffering that was associated with that detail was said to be 'willed' by Christ. Christ was in command, things were not happening to him randomly. The experiences of Christ's passion are then drawn on by the writer to be effective for their own life, particularly in the way of the forgiveness of sins.

Two other things struck me very forcibly at this stage: one was the detail of the subject matter, and the other was the emphasis on penitence. The detail of the subject matter was intensely close-in. If it were today, we should probably use a zoom lens on a camera. The writer takes, in a meditative way, an aspect of the body of Christ, which was not only involved in the suffering, but was also an integral part of the ministry. The eyes, for example, closed in death but open to the vision of God the Father; eyes which represented, in Jesus' ministry, the seeing of the truth of the Kingdom. So the closed eyes of Good Friday reflect back to the eyes which were such a fundamental reality of his earthly life, and were also an image of faith, 'if you have eyes to see, then see'.

I slowly began to get a feel for the mind of the writer, and would recognize the style, and so when other prayers from different manuscripts were compared there was a family likeness. I thought, at this time, that I was the only person in the world to know this manuscript, except of course for the long dead Messrs Bishop and Birch. That was until I decided to visit the British Museum Manuscripts Department, in order to look at and handle the real thing, the actual manuscript itself. Through all this I kept the nuns in mind, in order to keep my feet on the ground, to hold on to some sort of reality, and to the purpose behind all the searching for authorship. Prayers are for praying.

The Third Day of the Week. Our usual rations of food are cut right down this week, but I don't mind that too much. It won't be long before the great Paschal Feast. In fact, I'm beginning to think about that a bit too much as I try and pray. I find my mind wandering, and my stomach rumbling. The second, third and fourth days of the week are days Jesus spent teaching in the Temple, and then towards evening travelling back to Bethany, to the home of Mary, Martha and Lazarus. The more I think about the crucifixion the more I see it set in the context of this homely love Jesus experienced in Bethany. O yes, it was dark and cruel when it happened, but the love of it, and the love that surrounded him, mixed as it was with fear, and the love that was poured out.

THE BRITISH LIBRARY MANUSCRIPT DEPARTMENT

To handle a manuscript that was written at least before AD 900 is to enter a strange and awesome world. I bowled into the Manuscripts Room of the British Museum, having secured the necessary security paperwork, and wrote a request for the manuscript, *Harley 2965*. It was obviously one of their rarer manuscripts and so my case had to be scrutinized: 'Why do you want to see this particular manuscript?' Good question, why did I want to see it? Why was the Birch Hampshire Record Society publication not enough? On reflection it was because it contained prayers to a God I worship, about the death and passion of a Lord I hold dear, and whose death I take to be significant not only for myself but for the whole world. I wanted to see it because some anonymous scribe had taken the immense trouble to copy these prayers into a volume, along with the passion narratives from St Mark, St Luke, and St John, in a handwriting which I now know is called 'miniscules', and had illumined some of the letters, in not half as memorable a way as the Lindisfarne Gospels but very simply and at about the same time. I wanted to share in the immense pains taken to make these prayers available to men and women, most probably monks and nuns, to make their days leading up to the remembrance of the death of Christ helpful, meaningful and penitential. I wanted to come alongside Christ in these significant last few days of his life. I didn't actually say any of that to the Museum staff. I think I probably said that I was from Winchester, and the manuscript was of particular interest to me, and left it at that. But it was good enough to summon up the manuscript from the stacks. It also got me an introduction to one of the great scholars concerned with this manuscript, Michelle Brown, a curator of Western Manuscripts in the British Library, and author of *The Book of Cerne: Prayer, Patronage and Power in Ninth Century England*. It was she also who pointed me to the feminine aspects of the manuscript, and indirectly gave me the idea of interleaving this introduction with the thoughts of a female scribe.

The three other manuscripts which go together stylistically with the *Book of Nunnaminster* (London, British Library, Harley MS 2965), and which share similar material, are the *Book of Cerne* (Cambridge, University Library, MS L1.1.10), the *Royal Prayerbook* (London, British Library, Royal MS 2.A.xx) and the *Harleian Prayerbook* (London, British Library, Harley MS 7653). There are a variety of theories on their provenance, authorship and dating. Michelle Brown attributes the *Book of Cerne* to the powerful Anglo-Saxon Kingdom of Mercia, around 820–840. Its acrostic prayer attributed to King Aethelwold places it, according to another scholar, Dom A. B. Kuypers, in Lichfield.

We are peering into what has been termed the Dark Ages, but just to take these prayers as one example of what was coming out of the darkness gives us cause to redefine our understanding of the whole period. That there was danger from the Vikings is certainly true, but within that siege culture, and a time of great worldly uncertainty, there was produced a devotional literature which is still judged to be as imaginative and memorable as that of any period.

The Anglo-Saxons were not by any means monochrome peasants. They had a highly sophisticated cultural sense. Their jewellery was exquisite: see the workmanship of The Alfred Jewel kept in the Ashmolean Museum in Oxford, or the hoard from the Sutton Hoo Ship Burial in the British Museum. Their churches with their simple lines and their numinous, rounded arches helped Christian believers to enter into a new world, under them and through them.

The Feast Day of the Lord's Supper. Our usual times for our manual work are halted during this week. We have some very talented needleworkers, and I do some copying work. I have managed to complete the copying of the prayers for today. Today we have the service of the Last Supper, and the prayers we have been using and meditating on help us to think about Jesus giving his body as a remembrance: 'take, eat, this is my body' and again, 'this is the cup of my blood of the new covenant, which is for you and for many, poured out for the forgiveness of sins'. My prayer is that it will really help me be a better person, purer and holier, not so that I can lord it over all the others, but because, that way . . . why is it? . . . Is it just to get in closer to you, O my God . . . is it that everything else in comparison seems less important . . . fascinating and beautiful, but in the end, secondary . . . show me, O Lord, the one thing needful.

A COMBINATION OF CULTURES

We know a lot about the jewels and the silver of the Anglo-Saxon period, but what about the prayers? Through the prayers we look into a literary and spiritual world which combined several different cultures: the Irish-Celtic influence, the Roman and the Saxon. Each was strong, but the Irish influence is particularly interesting. In the Nunnaminster manuscript, as well as the passion prayers, and the Gospel Passion narratives, there is a 'breastplate' prayer, written probably by a seventh-century Irishman called Laidcenn, son of Prince Baeth. We are familiar with St Patrick's Breastplate which is a prayer for God to guard the believers from the enemy: behind, before, above, around. This 'breastplate' prayer of Laidcenn is a much more primitive, even superstitious, prayer asking God to protect a whole variety of different parts of the body, including the tongue, teeth, nostrils, neck, breast, side, entrails, thighs, bladder and many others. The Nunnaminster passion prayers, although included in the same manuscript, have a similar, although not so comprehensive, sense of the body. The great difference is that the corporal sense is linked to the gospel account of the death and suffering of Christ, and rather than just seeking for protection for the eyes or ears, these parts of the body become the springboard for an imaginative devotion to Christ himself and the power of his passion to release the sins committed by us through the eyes or ears, and other parts of our human body. Writing in that way is considered to be the effect of the Roman style combined with, or affected by, an Irish sensibility. The writings of the contemporary poet Seamus Heaney have this mixed cultural and stylistic quality. Indeed, in his book *Sweeney Astray* we are very much in the world of the Nunnaminster prayers, though the world is seen through the eyes of a wandering prince. One of the vivid images from the Prayers is that of sin entangling us like a thorn bush. Sweeney, in the poem 'Sweeney Astray', keeps getting tangled up in a hawthorn bush, both literally and also as a metaphor for a more general sense of confusion and distress.

A classic passage in Edmund Bishop's essay *An Ancient Manuscript*, referred to above, draws a helpful distinction between the Roman and the Irish-Celtic sensibilities in their style of writing prayers:

the Celt brings 'all heart' and much fluency with little mind, the Roman brings all mind and – I was going to say 'no' but had better perhaps prefer 'small' – heart.

The Anglo Saxon, in drawing on both, brought about a fusion of the two extremes, and in that fusion, or middle way, we see the beginnings of an 'English' quality in the prayers of this earliest devotional literature.

That is what makes these prayers so memorable. They have some of the imaginative flair of the Irish tradition which we see in theological writers and poets such as Sedulius Scotus (ninth century) and John Scotus Erigena (810–877), but they also have the restraint and shape of the Roman tradition of Alcuin. The prayers are after all written in Latin. Birch speaks of them as possessing 'an almost epigrammatic beauty of construction': a tradition we are familiar with in the Anglican tradition through the collects of the Book of Common Prayer, many of which are based on the Latin Sacramentaries of the fourth century.

This week is a heightening of everything: of a sense of bodily offering, with the fasting and the praying, but also out of the body, something completely spiritual. I move in and out of the bodily sense. As I kneel in prayer before the cross, at times I feel completely awkward, my legs, my head, my hands, and then for long periods it is as if I had no body. I think about the body of Christ, its weight on the cross, its weight taken from the cross, and then its resurrection lightness, its terrible obviousness on the cross, but how inaccessible, so untouchable. I think how irrelevant it is to what he was, and yet the look, the touch, the turn, the movement, the stillness . . . I am talking as if I was there. I know I wasn't. I'm here in the church, built in the shape of a cross. If I lie down and spread my arms, I am a little church, a humble cross, and I can carry Christ, hold him up to the world as Saviour.

THE CREATIVE CRUCIBLE

What crucible brought these different cultures together, leading up to the production of such exquisite prayers? One place was the eighth-century Carolingian court based at Liège, where Charlemagne encouraged a Christian learning and devotion which had such a great influence on the Church of those centuries. From that court was generated a whole new excitement for Christian teaching and learning, particularly under the inspiration of Alcuin of York (735–804) who Charlemagne brought over from Britain. Scriptural commentary, rhetoric and grammar, the arts of calligraphy and manuscript illumination, and poetry were all brought to a new pitch of excellence, and through this renaissance, new life was breathed into the tenth-century Benedictine tradition. New minsters were built, and the *Regularis Concordia*, detailing the liturgical patterns of the Benedictine life, was written in about 970.

In the aftermath of this renaissance, King Alfred encouraged learning and the translating of religious texts, and his connection with the monastic foundation of the Nunnaminster was extremely close. His sister Ealhswith founded it and was its principal patroness. We all know Alfred's reputation as a great king, but that kingship was based on a deep faith in God. He created a prayer book of his own in which he wrote prayers, which could be used at a moment's notice when he was entering the darkest periods of his own life:

> After learning poems by heart, he learnt the 'daily round', that is, the services of the hours, and then certain psalms and many prayers; these he collected in a single book, which he kept by him day and night, as I have seen for myself; amid all the affairs of the present life he took it around with him everywhere for the sake of prayer and was inseparable from it.
>
> (*Asser's Life of King Alfred* (Penguin 1983), p. 75 para. 24)

Alfred's little prayer book, or commonplace book of prayers, is just one more example of the interest there was in these times of gathering prayers for use on different occasions. In the biography of Alfred's life by Asser, this desire to collect 'flowers' of prayer and scripture was stimulated by the example of the penitent thief, for whom it was never too late to learn. The thief learnt his faith on the gallows, the king maintained his faith despite his busy daily life.

The more I read the passion story as told in the Gospel of St

John, the more I associate it with the Song of Songs. In John's Gospel we look at Christ with the eyes of love. No wonder Mary Magdalen plays such an important part in it. The pain is transformed by love. Love conquers death. Many waters cannot quench love. I go through all of this, not out of duty, but out of love, and not for some great ideal, but for a person. I wouldn't do it for anyone else, and doing it for someone I love makes all the routine glorious. But I am conscious of my unworthiness, the short shrift, the butterfly mind, the real horrible bits that I'm glad no one else can see. So my prayers are full of 'help', 'save', 'forgive', 'Lord, have mercy', groans too deep for words. Christ, you know all about it, come to me, your 'peccatrix', a sinner.

THE PRAYERS IN USE AT WINCHESTER

With the collection gathered here we must imagine a group of religious women, needing prayers for the observing of devotion to the cross, particularly in the weeks leading up to Easter, but also on Fridays and feasts concerned with the cross. They are members of the Order of St Benedict, and they are aware that throughout the country in the monasteries and convents of their order, literature is circulating to help them with their spiritual life. Among this material are prayers which would help them focus their devotion on the central feature of the gospel, the cross, and Jesus placed upon it. Copying prayers, like the making of garments and the embroidering of eucharistic vestments,

xxviii

were acts of love as well as of necessity. The Gospels, recounting the passion of Christ, and the prayers to say before the cross, are of particular importance. The ninth-century nuns of Winchester received these prayers from Worcester or Canterbury or Lichfield, in manuscript form, and they copied them. In the process of copying, the scribe, who was probably one of the nuns, replaced the male words with the female, and so 'sinner' sometimes changes from *peccator* to *peccatrix*. The prayer book stayed in the community, and on the spare pages at the back of it, at a later date, a map of the land owned by the *monasteriolum*, or 'little monastery', was drawn.

The prayers written within their own Benedictine tradition now became a central part of their own experience, as they used the prayers to mark the days before the annual remembrance of Christ's death on Good Friday, days in which they asked for particular grace and forgiveness, through the enabling power of God at work in Jesus.

These Anglo-Saxon nuns, and many like them throughout the country, lived in a world of strong contrasts. Life was full of beauty, captured in their love of artistic elaboration, colour and decoration, wall paintings, representations of the life and death of Christ. But it was also a life lived close to the bone of physical pain and ghostly fear. Within the monastic enclosure there was a reasonable sense of security, but hovering round was always the fear of foreign invasion, particularly from the Vikings. It was the age of Beowulf, as well as *The Dream of the Rood*. They were a pragmatic down to earth people, whose language is still well known for its bluntness. They were conscious of the physicality of their nature, its bodiliness, but also they were intensely devotional, and spiritual, closely in touch with the things of the world to come.

THE CRUCIFIED CHRIST

Into this world of contrasts was set their belief in God's saving power, and their devotion to the bodily presence of Jesus Christ, Lord and Saviour. Like us today, they had the Gospels to instruct and inspire them, and as something to imitate. The more I read commentaries on the Gospels the more amazing and numinous and central the actual gospel account of the crucifixion becomes. In a very real sense it is all there, and no more needs to be said. But the event has always laid itself open to retelling in word, picture, sculpture, music and drama. People have wanted to set their own mark upon it, to interpret it for themselves and their times and their communities, to make it their own. Pictures, or iconography, do this most vividly and accessibly. There the picture tells the old story, but retells it with individual emphasis: details which by their choice of what to put in and what to leave out tell an individual story. Which of the bystanders do they choose to include? Is Jesus dead, or dying, in pain, or in glory? Are the wounds added? Is he slumped or straight? Does the Holy Spirit, in the form of a dove, hover over the cross? Visual representations of the crucifixion have their own dialect.

xxx

A prayer based on the crucifixion has another individual dialect. A prayer only has words at its disposal, and those words have to describe, and bring into relation, the writer, and God, and the victim of the passion. How does this writer do the job? What is it about the prayers that are so attractive and compelling, and makes them by their style and their intent so contemporary?

The Jesus of these prayers is not a lone, individual figure, redeeming the world. He is going the way of the cross with the Father's almighty power and protection surrounding him. In addition, then, the writer focuses our thoughts on the tangible, the real, the human aspect of Jesus. The body of Jesus is the one thing that could not bypass human suffering and death. He could not turn into an angel, or a ghost, and evade the sheer humanness of pain and humiliation. It is the body of Jesus to which these prayers direct their primary focus. They are tangible images. We see the eyes which close, the neck which has the cross fixed on it and which bears the weight of the wood, the ears which hear the appeal of the penitent thief, the hands bored through with nails.

Yet it does not just stop there. The body, the humanness, is a means through to the spiritual. It is by physical suffering that authority and power emanates to effect the spiritual life of the one praying, be it freedom from guilt or protection from evil, or a request to share in the life of the saints in heaven. This meeting of the physical and the spiritual is what is meant by the word 'incarnational'. God took on a body, living among the world he had created, in order to transform human potential so that it could participate in the divine.

The tone of the prayers is unique. They are a special mixture of the personal and the theological. Written earlier they might not have had the vocabulary of the human heart; written later they might not have been able to escape sentimentality. They hit that clearest, most melodious note: true to the spirit of the gospel, sharp with the insights of Paul's redemption theology, and with just a breath of the personal imagination writing its signature in the thorn bush of sin, and the drowsy prayer-time.

Tell them about the love, how it shines like the spring sun. Tell them about the purity and the joy with which the water jumbles over the chalk bed of the river. Tell them about the night sky and the clarity of the stars, under whose canopy and in whose friendly darkness I make my way to pray in the middle of the night. Tell them how, when I listen in the silence, there is the sound of the one bird singing. Tell them of the ringing bell that marks the movement of the day. Tell them of the moment when the sun just catches my back after a long winter. Tell them of the flowers, the early ones, the tough and beautiful ones. Tell them how all those things are patches in the patchwork of the great Paschal Feast. Tell them how a dying is a rising, and a saving.

The anonymous nun, the scribe of the prayers, the sinner who is a woman, reminds me that I have omitted to talk of one important feature of these prayers, and that is 'love'. The love in which the incidents are described, and by which love is further engendered in the one praying, has a quality about it which takes us almost straight to the biblical book the Song of Songs, which is why wherever possible I have used a bridging quotation from the Song between the prayer and the meditation. The prayers are without a hint of sentimentality, although it was very difficult to find a better translation for 'dulcis' and 'venerabile', than sweet and lovely. This love has a mystical quality, and all the best mystical writings are as tough as leather, and are rooted in a good day's gardening, or washing, or baking. Such was the life of the Benedictine convent in which these prayers were used.

We forget in our spiritual lives that without a body we would not be anything. The love that pervades these prayers is an enfleshed love, it is body speaking to body, longing for that physicality to reach its natural sinless perfection, in the resurrection from the dead. A state, or a life, which will not blur the person, body and soul, but regenerate the unified being into a communion with all the saints. It is so easy for passion prayers to tip over into maudlin sentimentality, or a gruesome perspective, or into soul-less theology. The virtue of these prayers is their balance, held between the verbal equivalents of body, mind and spirit.

The Prayers

1

ON THE BENDING OF THE KNEE

O tremendous God, adored, revered,
to you every knee shall bend
in heaven, on earth and under the earth,
but you, Lord, in your compassion
bend your own knees
and indeed with all the joints in your body
have willed to fix your gaze on God
pleading with your Father.
I thank you
and by the life-giving drops of your holy sweat
grant me forgiveness,
and whenever I set aside my prayer
or become drowsy with sleep,
and hedged about with the sloth of my body;
hold me in the company of those
for whom you knock against
the ears of your Father in prayer,
and not by my merits, but by your mercy,
Lord Jesus Christ,
Amen.

I sleep, but my heart waketh: it is the voice of my beloved that knocketh, saying, Open to me, my sister, my love, my dove, my undefiled.

(Song of Solomon 5.2)

All prayer begins in adoration to God: a turning to God in one's heart, and a turning outwards in acknowledgement of God's power, which is above all that we can summon from our own earthly strength. We only have to think, for a moment, of our inability to create ourselves, or to avoid the inevitable point of death, to be led into an understanding of God's creative power. The tremendous God is to be adored, revered and approached in awesome wonder.

I find it difficult to launch into a time of prayer with God from cold, immediately to feel awe without something to spark it off, but if we wait for our emotional state to be ready then we could wait a long time. For so many, for so long, it has been the act of kneeling which has set the body, and so the soul, into an attitude of prayer. This is not the only physical position that is possible or even helpful, sitting, standing, dancing, whirling, standing on your head even, are all possible, and can be explored, but the obeisance of the knee sets up the physical relationship of servant to Lord, which is not a bad beginning for us and God. Then, an act of the will: 'I want to be with God. I long to be in the presence of God.' The Holy Spirit is the great ally of the will, the great

4

energizer of prayer, and calling on the Holy Spirit to assist our human will is a very good beginning.

Think of Jesus in Gethsemane. He knelt down before his Father and prayed. He prayed so earnestly 'the sweat was like drops of blood falling to the ground'. He prayed first that the inevitable course of suffering, symbolized by the cup, should be taken away, but this prayer was later discarded to be replaced by 'your will be done', the second petition of the Lord's Prayer.

In the account of the night of prayer in Gethsemane in St Luke's Gospel, Jesus finds his disciples asleep, and he is dismayed that they could not keep awake at such an important time in the approach of God's Kingdom. Sloth affects all of us in our life of prayer. We give up praying, we prefer to do other things, it slips out of our timetable, we get too tired, we leave it to moments when our body is unable to be of help to our spirit.

Christ the great intercessor will help us. We need only ask. 'Ask, and you will receive; seek, and you will find; knock, and the door will be opened to you' (Matthew 7.7). He will pray for us to his Father, in the power of the Holy Spirit. He will knock at the door of his Father's heart and it will open gladly to him, and we shall enter too, not on our own merits, but by the saving mercy of Christ.

2

ON THE KISS OF JUDAS

Holy, invisible and incomprehensible God,
who, by the traitor Judas
was betrayed with a kiss,
you gave yourself into hostile hands,
confronted your enemies
and defending your disciples, said,
'I am the one. Let them be!'
You gave them your hands
so they could fasten you by your flesh,
you, who had no power to harm.
By all of this
I beseech you on my knees
to defend me against my enemies,
and to release the works of my hands
from the chains of sin,
Lord Jesus Christ,
Amen.

Let him kiss me with the kisses of his mouth.
(Song of Solomon 1.2)

The kiss is a sign of peace and love. It evokes an intimacy and a closeness which demands an ability to give and to receive beyond almost any other greeting. It signs and seals friendship. It says 'I love you. I trust you.' There is nothing to say that this kiss by Judas was on the lips or on the cheek, or whether it was an embrace, but the irony of the act of the kiss in Gethsemane has not been lost on readers of the Gospels in which it was recorded. The sign of friendship becomes the traitor's ruse. The seal of love becomes the seal of Jesus' destiny.

The handing over, or betrayal, of Jesus is willed by him. In these prayers there is always a strong sense that nothing happens to Jesus which is outside his will: 'you who willed that . . .' is a constant refrain. Jesus is never out of control. The passion is more than just voluntarily taken on. The God who is over all, through all and in all is willing to go the way of suffering, and to go victoriously. It is of his own choosing and, in some strange way, of his own making.

The binding and arrest of Christ is a binding of his flesh, his Spirit is inviolable. He is taken prisoner in the only way possible, which is the way of the flesh. By the binding of Jesus, he is able to save those bound by 'the chains of sin', for the word of God is not fettered (2 Timothy 2.9) and he is able to take captivity captive, both cosmically and in a personal sense. The one who was himself bound is able to loose us from the thraldom of sin, and bind us together again with love (Colossians 3.14).

3

ON RESTORING THE EAR

God,
whose good favour none can do without
and who has taught us the forgiveness of sins:
how greatly you showed an example of kindness
when, after it was cut off,
you restored the High Priest's servant's ear,
I give you thanks
and by this,
I plead with you,
depart from me sinner that I am.
If in whatever way I have sinned
by word or deed or in retaining a memory,
or in rejoicing in the evil of one
or not rejoicing in the good of another,
forgive those things, O mighty one,
and by this make me perfect,
Lord Jesus Christ,
Amen.

Thou that dwellest in the gardens, the companions hearken to thy voice: cause me to hear it.

(Song of Solomon 8.13)

One of the main ways of receiving the word of God is to hear it, and the complaints of the prophets, Isaiah in particular, were that the people would hear the spoken word with their outward ear, but it would not penetrate more deeply:

> (The Lord) replied: 'Go tell this people:
>   However hard you listen, you will never understand
>   However hard you look, you will never perceive.
>   The people's wits are dulled;
>   they have stopped their ears and shut their eyes,
>   so that they may not see with their eyes
>   nor listen with their ears,
>   nor understand with their wits,
>   and then turn and be healed.'

(Isaiah 6.9–10)

For the deaf to hear is a great miracle, not only because sound itself is so precious, but because then the word of God can be heard and heeded. So we recall the healing of Malchus' ear, cut off in an act of bravado by one of the disciples in the Garden of Gethsemane. Jesus showed his compassion even at this late stage by restoring the ear: 'Love your enemies, do good to those who hate you.' How he did that, we do not know: why he did it, we can understand. This is the one who restores the capacity to hear and see, to walk, to live with a new vigour and purpose, and with the ear and the heart restored they join together in the act of listening.

To listen to God, and to listen to our conscience, that is the task of the restored inward ear. That, in turn, allows us to hear the needs of our neighbours, and to assess whether we are 'retaining a memory . . . rejoicing in the evil of one, or not rejoicing in the good of another', and to seek for forgiveness, and perfection from our Lord, Jesus Christ. To listen with the inward ear, listening deeply to God, we need first to be touched with the healing power of Christ. Once healed, we are all ears.

4

ON THE JUDGEMENT OF THE GOVERNOR

You, who judge all in fairness,
and heard the unfair judgement of a judge,
I thank you, plead with you,
and humbly ask you, in your mercy,
to grant that I may never hear
the judgement of eternal condemnation,
and in that joyful future time
you may keep from your mouth
the harshest words,
Lord Jesus Christ,
Amen.

His mouth is most sweet . . . this is my beloved, and this is my friend.

(Song of Solomon 5.16)

The deep issues in the passion keep surfacing. The one who knows more than any other what is in a person, and courts no one's favour, is himself under judgement by Pilate (John 18.28–38). It is Jesus who at the end of time, like the Son of Man, will be at the right hand of God to call for mercy on all those whose lives have showed mercy on others. He will do this with 'his sweet mouth'.

But here that advocate has no defence other than the truth: 'My task is to bear witness to the truth. For this I was born; for this I came into the world, and all who are not deaf to truth listen to my voice' (John 18.37). The claims of kingship which the Jews accuse Jesus of, and Pilate questions him about, are neither here nor there in the light of the truth. Yet the one who shows mercy also has the power to condemn. The one would be meaningless without the other. Jesus condemns evil, hatred, pride, adultery, hypocrisy and lack of charity, and has harsh words to say about them and those who perpetrate them, but he offers an alternative way in love, mercy, kindness, honesty and peacefulness.

Jesus gives, through repentance, a way out to freedom for those who have become deeply embedded in the ways which lead away from God. The writer of this prayer knows that the first door to knock on for this forgiveness and mercy is the door of Christ himself. The face of Christ, and his sweet mouth, in the icon paintings of the Eastern Orthodox tradition are pictured as both infinitely compassionate and yet also strong. We are challenged by the searching eyes and the firm, sweet mouth of the one who judges in all fairness.

5

ON DIVERSE PASSIONS

God, my God,
I am your servant
and I never cease to thank you
and rightly so
because you have willed to bear
on my behalf, the evil of the hands
of those that beat you.
What stripes,
what bonds,
what spit,
what blows,
what hatred, and false evidence:
and by all these things I implore you
to take away from me the thongs
and chains of my enemies,
and by the fire of your love,
and by the spit on your face,
purge me and sanctify me,
from all the sins and the crimes
that are in me,
Lord Jesus Christ,
Amen.

15

Set me as a seal upon thine heart, as a seal upon thine
arm: for love is strong as death; jealousy is cruel as the
grave: the coals thereof are coals of fire, which hath a most
vehement flame.

(Song of Solomon 8.6)

In Bishop Lancelot Andrewes' private notebook of prayers, he
made a list of all the sufferings of Christ mentioned in the
Gospels. With one or two overlaps there are 107 in the list from
'the constraining desire' of the baptism Christ longed to under-
go but had to wait for, to the blood and water flowing from his
side, which, since it followed his death, perhaps cannot be
classified as a suffering. The sufferings were many and diverse,
and concentrated into a brief span from Gethsemane to Calvary,
and they were willed to be suffered on our behalf. He willed to
be 'pierced for our transgressions' (Isaiah 53.5).

The sufferings mentioned in this prayer are confined to those
administered by the Imperial Guard, and by attendants at the
high priest's house; which are severe enough. They include the
beatings, stripes and blows: with fists in the high priest's house,
and with sticks in Pilate's guardroom. The spit is in the high
priest's court. The 'vincula', the bonds, come from John 18.24,
'So Annas sent him bound to Caiaphas the high priest'; and the
false evidence is from the court of Caiaphas: 'Many gave false
evidence against him' (Mark 14.56).

Christ's suffering is a channel of prayer to God, by which the enemies' binding of us can be released. We can be purged by the fire of his love and sanctified by the spit he received, which was not only the means of Christ's healing the deaf-mute, but was also the spit received in the high priest's tribunal.

The 'fire of Christ's love' is a powerful phrase, and is a strong link between the passion narrative and our reading of the Song of Songs. Christ is betrothed to us in love through suffering, and the cross is the sign and seal of that commitment.

6

THE CROWN OF THORNS

Merciful God,
my helper,
you did not refuse to wear
a crown of thorns
on your wise and lovely head.
I thank you
and whatever sins
I have at any time committed
by the senses
of my wicked and senseless head;
forgive me, because I am
inflicted by the sharpness
of almost every wrongdoing,
as if by thorns,
unless I am protected by your help,
Lord Jesus Christ,
Amen.

His head is as the most fine gold, his locks are bushy, and black as a raven.

(Song of Solomon 5.11)

Thorns and thickets are images of the sharp points and entangling arms of the sins which we commit. What thorns surround us, that strangle the word of God and wither it within us! Some seed falls among thorns, as the parable of the sower reminds us (Mark 4.7) and chokes the corn, and it produces no crop. To get tangled up, entangled in things that do us no good, is a familiar part of most of our journeys.

In the ancient Irish writings of the centuries in which these prayers were written, to fall into a hawthorn bush was an image of despair. The thorns were the claws of death. To be caught in them was to be an outcast, pulled from the heights to the depths. The thick brown jaggy hawthorns of Ireland, tumbled into in childhood adventures, become the much deeper and thicker problems of adult life.

God, our helper and protector in this dense undergrowth, himself wore a crown of thorns on his wise and lovely head. The head, which is the crown of the body, was given a cruel crown of thorns. The seat of wisdom which makes the head venerable, the root of compassion and beauty which makes it precious, lovely and revered, is bowed before the world and crowned with thorns. Christ is the head, and on that head we depend. From it all our needs are supplied. By Christ's head we are all knit together into one body (Colossians 2.19).

Yet, it is the crown of thorns which helps us with our thorns: 'As the lily among thorns, so is my love' (Song of Songs 2.2). As the lily stands out in purity and beauty among the thorns, so Christ's love signals to us through the pain and suffering of the cross. The beauty of his life, its moral and spiritual perfection, cannot be spoilt by torture or humiliation. He takes on the deepest suffering of humanity so that we never need to feel alone in ours. Those things which have got me in their grip, and in which I am all tangled up, are released by the wearer of the crown of thorns.

What are the 'senses' of the head? The head contains the brain, the thoughts, the computer. It is the image-maker, the decision-maker. In the head we shape our being human. To be aware of the sense that we can make, or the nonsense, is a great responsibility: many things will want to knock us off the branch into the thickets and thorns below. So we call on the head of Christ to help, to help us put on his mind, to mind his way.

7

ON THE DERISION OF THE LORD

God,
whose loving power and majesty
the hymn-singing choir of angels
unceasingly worships,
and yet, under derision from men,
you, the adored one, keep silent;
I thank you,
and beg you,
by the effective clemency of your prayers,
for your true forbearance;
so that whenever I call on you
with heartfelt requests,
may your merciful ears hear them,
Lord Jesus Christ,
Amen.

I sought him, but I could not find him; I called him, but he gave me no answer.

(Song of Solomon 5.6)

The two opposite themes of this prayer are derision and praise. The hymn-singing choir of angels are set against the derision of the people at the crucifixion, and the still centre of this see-saw of praise and derision is the silent Christ.

Angels have always been musical figures. They joined in with the heavenly host singing 'Glory to God in the highest heaven' at the birth of Jesus (Luke 2.14). The seraphim surround the Lord in Isaiah's temple vision (Isaiah 6.2, 3) and call 'Holy, holy, holy is the Lord of Hosts: the whole earth is full of his glory'. The angels are to praise God, as well as being his messengers, and they praise God with a great acclamation of his glory.

In stark contrast at the crucifixion of Jesus, there are shouts and jeers of derision. Some cried out 'Prophesy!' in the High Priest's hurriedly convened trial in the temple; in Pilate's guard room the soldiers knelt and paid mock homage to Jesus (Mark 15.19). The passers-by wagged their heads and jeered at Jesus as he hung on the cross: '"Bravo!" they cried, "So you are the man who was to pull down the temple, and rebuild it in three days! Save yourself and come down from the cross"' (Mark 15.29). To all of this Jesus responds with a compassionate silence. The time of his verbal teaching is over. His death is now both his sermon and his willingness to go the way that leads to salvation for the world. Jesus bore the insults and the jeers, he did not cut himself off from them. He took them to himself, and asked his Father to forgive those who were instrumental in his suffering.

His ears and his heart remained open to his torturers, as they remain open to our prayers today. We may not see ourselves as torturers in the conventional sense, but we still remain in need of God's forgiveness, his forbearance, and we still look to God for help in our lives, as we come to him with our requests.

8

ON THE LORD'S CROSS

Lord Jesus,
only source and summit of our prayer,
you did not refuse
to hold and to carry
the burden of the cross,
by which you raised up
the sins of the human race
and put that heavy burden
on your own shoulders,
as the immaculate lamb would do.
I pray to you
to stretch out the hand of pity to me
for I am tangled up in all the sins of the world,
and loose me
from the thickets of sin
and lift me out of them.
Lord Jesus Christ,
Amen.

Go forth, O ye daughters of Zion, and behold king Solomon with the crown wherewith his mother crowned him in the day of his espousals, and in the day of the gladness of his heart.

(Song of Solomon 3.11)

To shoulder the cross is a phrase which evokes the physicality of the burden very vividly. We can feel its weight pressing down on our own shoulders, like a heavy backpack after a day's walking, or as the shoulders of our ancestors would have felt yoked to pails of water or milk, or as refugees carrying their possessions along the roads. We can imagine Christ carrying the cross, and we can feel it.

St John is the only one of the evangelists to say specifically that Jesus carried the cross himself (John 19.17). The first three evangelists share the memory of Simon of Cyrene assisting Jesus when he stumbled, by shouldering the cross for him (Matthew 27.32; Mark 15.21; Luke 23.26).

The weight of the cross is here increased by the symbolic load of sin. It was weighted down with the sin of the human race, and it was Jesus who took that weight on his own shoulders in carrying the cross. He bore our sins, bore their weight, bore the responsibility, bore the pain and the shame of them, and was killed for them. Under the old covenant, the pure and spotless lamb took on those burdens.

The theme of the prayer is influenced by the story in Genesis

22.13. The carrying of the wood up the mountain by Isaac, its significance initially unknown to him, in preparation for the sacrifice, gives the imaginative lead, and the writer of the prayer feels himself to be the ram caught in the thicket by its horns, longing for release.

The images are jumping about here quite a lot, never staying still for very long, but the final image remains. It is of Jesus lifting us, out of the thicket of sin and wrongdoing, freeing us from the tangle and mess of our own making, by our appeal to him for help:

I pray to you to stretch out the hand of pity to me.

To stretch out is to offer, and that can be seen as the same offering that Jesus made in the Last Supper, when he took bread, blessed, broke and offered it, to his disciples and to us.

9

ON HIS CLOTHES

O protector God,
and defender of my life,
you would never discard the garments
of your goodness.
You allowed your perfect body
to be shamefully stripped
so that the nakedness of the first man
could be redeemed.
I thank you,
and by that being stripped
loose me I pray
from the misery of sin,
and so clothe me
that at the entrance to the Kingdom
I shall not be naked but clothed
with the wedding garment
of your life-giving goodness.
Lord Jesus Christ,
Amen.

The watchmen that went about the city found me, they smote me, they wounded me; the keepers of the walls took away my veil from me.

(Song of Solomon 5.7)

The earliest reference to clothes in the Bible comes in the context of shame. Adam and Eve's joint involvement with disobedience to the will of God, has made them ashamed of their nakedness, and 'so they stitched fig-leaves together and made themselves loin-cloths' (Genesis 3.7). For some deep psychological reason our paradisal nakedness is not a comfortable state. Whether that is because of a long tradition of clothes worn for warmth and protection in a cold and hostile environment, or is reflective of a break with the will of God at some point in human development, and has continued in us ever since, it is difficult to know. The fault line runs through every human being.

So when Jesus was stripped of his clothes (Matthew 27.28; Mark 15.17; John 19.2), or of the seamless garment (John 19.23), he took on both the paradisal state of Adam and the shame of nakedness which was keenly felt by the Jews. Although his outward garment went, that did not mean that the garments of righteousness were taken away (Isaiah 61.10).

With the writers' customary way of dealing in typology – which is one thing reflecting or being the type of another – here, in a reverse way, Jesus' nakedness was a way of allowing the nakedness of Adam to be redeemed. Jesus went back to the place where Adam was before his disobedience, sanctified it, owned it once again, and made it holy.

But this was not the end. The natural paradisal nakedness had to be reclothed, to be made suitable for the Kingdom (Matthew 22.11). The wedding garment had to be put on by Christ. That wedding garment was a garment of light, of a brightness no earthly washing could produce. It was a body transfigured by grace.

This is not 'a body beautiful' in the modern sense of beautiful to the eye, or merely aesthetically well proportioned, but a body, and particularly the face (Mark 9.3), which is luminous. It is illuminated by the good things which have been taught and done, and because the life has been lived along the grain of God's will. So the Kingdom is approached.

10

PRAYER OF THE NECK

Fountain of all goodness
and form of true humility,
you
bent your holy neck
and let a cross be placed on you.
I thank you
and with the neck of my heart bent low,
grant me, unworthy of glory,
forgiveness of sins,
and equality with the most faithful of saints,
Lord Jesus Christ,
Amen.

Thy neck is like the tower of David builded for an armoury, whereon there hang a thousand bucklers, all shields of mighty men.

(Song of Solomon 4.4)

The neck holds the mind to the heart, the brain to the belly. It is a bridge, a channel, and therefore it is a place of vulnerability and the point of execution. It is also beautiful and sensitive, on which are hung jewels and honours. Jesus 'bent his holy neck' to have the cross placed upon it, and so we bend our necks low, in unworthiness, pleading for the forgiveness of sins and a place alongside the saints.

Those who did not bend to the will of God were called 'stiff-necked', those who looked down on others 'proud-necked'. But there is a rightful pride in carrying the head which is drawn up to God, which is leading the way to heaven, and has hung on it the spoils of the victory of the war fought for God and his Kingdom.

In this prayer, the neck is the place of humility. All that makes us great and powerful in the eyes of the world and in our own minds we offer in humility to God. In our bowing we offer to God our whole being, our selves, all that we are and all that we ever hope to be.

11

OF HIS ARMS AND HANDS

O right hand of God,
and giver of salvation,
your holy arms were stretched out
on the wood of the cross;
your great, holy and lovely hands
were pierced through
with the marks of the nails.
I thank you Lord Jesus Christ
and pray,
plead to you, to reach out
those hands of mercy to me,
and with the sharp point of fear and love
to pierce this most hardened heart of mine,
and to direct, guide and guard
the works of my hands.
Do not despise me as unworthy
of the work of your hands,
Lord Jesus Christ,
Amen.

His left hand is under my head, and his right hand doth embrace me.

(Song of Solomon 2.6)

'These arms', says Jesus, 'are stretched out to embrace the whole world. They are open for you, and you, and open with such poverty no one is too poor or too wicked to be gathered in, and I will keep them wide open for ever. This is the last picture you will have of me in my complete humanity, and every time you look at the crucifix, at the cross, you will be able to say, "they are spread for me". And the cross stretches to the north of the north, and to the very south of the south, and to east and west, until the arms meet again and join around the whole world, and all the world can be embraced.'

'Come to me, all who are weary and whose load is heavy; I will give you rest' (Matthew 11.28). 'Let the children come to me; do not try to stop them' (Matthew 19.14). 'Father, forgive them' (Luke 23.34). All are welcome into the Kingdom, but not all will come, and so we need to plead with Christ to show our love for him, and to share our conscious need of mercy. His arms are held out in love for us, he longs for us to return that love and to hold out our arms to him, saying 'Yes, we believe and trust in you as our redeemer and saviour'.

The nails which pierced the hands of Christ can also pierce our hearts to make them sensitive, and pliable in the service of the Lord. The piercing of the heart was the destiny of Mary, prophesied by Simeon (Luke 2.34). Whoever wishes to save his life will lose it, whoever loses his life for the sake of Jesus will save it. The calling to break our hearts in the communities we serve is a very hard lesson to learn:

> sorrow may bud the tree with tears,
> But only his blood can make it bloom.
> (R. S. Thomas, 'The Tree')

How strange that the most powerful, effective and creative work of Christ in redeeming the world was done with pinioned hands. We might think that absurd. We would need all our limbs in full working order to do what we have to do, but not Christ. It was in obedience to the will of God that the redemptive power was released. He gave up his will, which included giving up his freedom and mobility, so that having offered everything over, God could be through and through the one who acts. In Christ's weakness was his strength: bound himself, he could free others; a prisoner, he could liberate the world (2 Corinthians 6.3–10)

12

ON THE SEVEN GIFTS OF THE HOLY SPIRIT

O, intimate, merciful, redeemer God
whose sevenfold gifts of the Holy Spirit,
and eightfold blessings,
are both kept within your heart
and offered out, without demanding return:
I thank you,
and pray to you
most high God,
to take from my heart
the eightfold great sins,
and from all the uncleanness of sin,
purify me, body and soul,
you
who have lit up, with all virtue,
the pure and the strong.
Lord Jesus Christ,
Amen.

Because of the savour of thy good ointments thy name is as ointment poured forth.

(Song of Solomon 1.3)

All blessings and all gifts come from God, as well as the virtues: wisdom, understanding, counsel, fortitude, knowledge, piety and the fear of the Lord (Isaiah 11.2, 3). They come from God, but God holds onto them so that they are always available. He is the source of them all, the source which never runs dry, but always bubbles up with goodness, with things that bring and maintain life. He is 'the author and giver of all good things'.

The numbers seven and eight have been used for all sorts of lists of things, both good and bad. The gifts of the Holy Spirit are often seen as the sacraments: baptism, confirmation, marriage, ordination, chrism, penance and unction. The eightfold blessings referred to in the prayer are probably the Beatitudes of Matthew 5.1–10, addressed to the poor, sorrowful, gentle, hungry and thirsty, merciful, pure, peacemakers and persecuted.

Set against these virtues, sacraments and blessings are the seven deadly sins: pride, lust, covetousness, envy, gluttony, anger, sloth, accidie or dejection. 'Take from my heart the eightfold great sins' is a fine sentiment, but what that actually means in practice depends on how we make decisions and sum up the ways of the world. Living a life which is free of pride and lust takes most people years of practice, but we have to start somewhere.

Take pride, for example, the 'lion of pride', as the twelfth-century Anchorites' Rule puts it: not to take undue concern in our own success, not even to see it as success; to embrace all that helps us be humble, without knowing that that is what we are doing; not to be other than what God has made us be, where we are, satisfied that what is, is enough. The words are nothing until they take on meaning from our own scrutiny of ourselves.

13

AGAIN CONCERNING
THE SUFFERING OF THE CROSS

Lifter up of the lowly
and strength of the frail,
who in your weakness
raised a fallen world
and let yourself in your humility
be lifted up by the corrupt hands of sinners
onto the cross.
I give you thanks,
and by this act
I pray that you,
who did not neglect the one lost sheep,
but having found it,
lifted it onto your sinless shoulders
and brought it back into the fold,
may think it worthy
to lift me from earth to heaven,
Lord Jesus Christ,
Amen.

Who is she that looketh forth as the morning, fair as the
moon, clear as the sun, and terrible as an army with
banners?

(Song of Solomon 6.10)

The lifting up of the tokens of power of commitment or allegiance
seems to be common in many cultures or religions. In the desert,
Moses lifted up the bronze serpent as a source of healing; and
so the cross, itself a symbol of cruelty and destruction, was set
up, with Christ nailed to it, to overcome destruction and to defeat
death. Totem poles, as banners, are built high to declare an allegiance, and so the Christian Church sings 'Lift high the cross'.
The *vexilla regis*, or 'the standard of the king', must be raised in
battle, as a rallying point, a sign of purpose, and something to
raise the hearts of the soldiers. So the cross is the rallying point
in our battle, against the forces that destroy the light of love,
that reject the creative forces of God, and for Christ who only
has the power to save.

What sort of a saviour is this? He is the Good Shepherd, who
sets out at night to find the lost sheep (Luke 15.4–6) and brings
it home to safety, warmth and companionship, to where it
belongs. The picture of the shepherd with the sheep round his
shoulders, with its hooves firmly held in one hand and the crook
in the other, is an abiding one, and one very resonant of the
searching kindness of Christ himself. He set out to find the lost
sheep of the house of Israel: which meant those burdened by

the law, ostracized by the society of his day, by illness, disease or poverty. Christ the Good Shepherd was also moved by the charity of the Samaritans and the perception of the Syro-Phoenician woman who, like the dog with material crumbs under the table, would be pleased to pick up the spiritual crumbs from the table of her Lord.

This is the Good Shepherd who is committed to his sheep, his people, and is prepared to lay down his life for them on the cross. The sheep across the shoulders is removed and is replaced by the wood of the cross, so that we who are lost may be raised up and brought home.

14

ON DARKNESS

Merciful and powerful,
praised and honoured in all things,
your passion affected the whole world.
In your wounding
the elements were shaken.
The day was terrified by this most unusual night
and the world discovered shadows;
the light was seen to die with you
so that you could not be seen
by those who had committed a sacrilege.
The eyes of heaven were shut
because they could not bear
to look at you on the cross:
I pray for them to you as Saviour of the world.
By the passion and the redemption
of your saving cross
take from me this earthly house that is my body.
Send an angel of peace and consolation
to protect me from the crowds of enemies
whose only desire is to slay souls.
Guard my soul and keep it fearless

through the princedoms and the powers
and lead me to the shining seats,
and this I ask
not for any merit of mine
but nor do I despair of reaching you
by your mercy and with your protection,
Lord Jesus Christ,
Amen.

Until the day break, and the shadows flee away, turn, my
beloved, and be thou like a roe or a young hart upon the
mountains of Bether.

(Song of Solomon 2.17)

There are two sorts of darkness. There is the darkness that is
opposed to light, that tries to overcome it, extinguish it, banish
it; and there is the darkness that is the inevitable result of trying
to see and understand a God who is beyond our understanding.

St Paul talked to the Galatians of powers which worked
against light and goodness. He called them 'the elemental
powers of the universe', which in themselves had no power to
save. However great and awesome the created world may be,
there existed a neutrality deep within it which always left it
radically disjointed from the human world made in the image of
God. The extent to which we are a part of the elemental spirits

of the universe is a matter of scientific debate. We are certainly made from the same materials, the same elements, but we are not neutral. We have a free will, engendered by God, by which he gave us the power to love him or reject him.

'The elemental spirits' of Paul's world were shaken by the crucifixion, turned upside down. Day became night, and darkness covered the land. Darkness came for shame on those who had crucified Jesus, and so they were unable to see the act they had perpetrated. Darkness came as a relief, because the eyes of heaven could not bear to look at the crucified Christ.

In a world without electric light, the darkness would have been far deeper and more debilitating and terrifying, and light would have been far more of a relief. The unknown, mysterious presences would easily be designated evil, as projections of fear. To know all is to love all, but in our ignorance now and still we fear things in others, and we fear unknown things in ourselves. So we pray to God, 'guard our souls and keep us fearless'. We fear the terrible power of nations who are set for war (Ephesians 6.12), and for the forces of evil which build up and attack us. So we set prayer against the evil forces, and do not give up hope.

15

ON THE THIEF

My Lord God,
who desires not the death of a sinner
but penitence,
and who promised paradise
to the thief who showed that he had faith,
throw open the hope of forgiveness
to us penitents as well;
and so I give you thanks
and call on your mercy,
and confess to you my wickedness:
what I have done by my mouth, my heart,
my deeds, and in all those things that
I have brought shame upon myself,
I seek forgiveness
so that you may blot out all my sins,
Lord Jesus Christ,
Amen.

Awake, O north wind; and come, thou south; blow upon my garden, that the spices thereof may flow out. Let my beloved come into his garden, and eat his pleasant fruits.

(Song of Solomon 4.16)

The reward for faith, even at the last hour, is paradise. We might have expected the Kingdom as the meeting place with Jesus after death, but he uses the more general and popular 'paradise'. In the story of Genesis, man and woman started in paradise. It was pictured as a garden, full of beautiful things, natural and abundant things: trees, rivers, flowers and animals; but the disobedience of humanity spoilt it and caused its own banishment. Ever since then there has been a nostalgia to return to the garden, to paradise.

'Kindness is a paradise in its blessings,' writes the author of Ecclesiasticus (40.17). Paul knew a man who was caught up into paradise and heard words so secret that human lips may not repeat them (2 Corinthians 12.4). St John writes to the church at Ephesus: 'To those who are victorious I will give the right to eat from the tree of life that stands in the garden of God' (Revelation 2.7). But the paradise is complete for the repentant and faithful criminal because he will be with Christ in paradise, he will live for ever in the new garden, free of his sins, with his saviour.

It was no easy confession. The criminal was on the cross, a time when self-concern would be at its height, but he acknowledges both his own fault, the rightness of the judgement upon him, and the innocence of Christ. That extremely difficult leap into penitence, the acknowledgement of one's own failure and the confession of it, deserves the reward. He achieved it through the forgiving power of Christ, who shared the plight of that same crucifixion.

16

ON THE VINEGAR AND THE GALL

Lord God of hosts, and God of all the earth,
in your mouth, full of honour,
you have opened the way of life and truth to all
and did withstand the bitterness
of vinegar and gall
by the sweet precepts for life;
and you have tasted the bitterness
with spotless lips
and did reject it from your mouth:
take the bitterness of eternal death
far from me and from everyone.
Hear me,
Eternal God,
in my prayer and in my thanksgiving,
that by whatever evil is in my mouth,
whatever oath or slander, lies or false witness,
whatever vanity of speech by which I have sinned,
all these may be sent back from you
into their opposite,
and not because I deserve it,
but because you are generous in your mercy,
Lord Jesus Christ,
Amen.

Take us the foxes, the little foxes, that spoil the vines: for our vines have tender grapes.

(Song of Solomon 2.15)

The memory of the sour wine has gone through some complicated and subtle changes. Psalm 69.21 stands at the fount of the tradition:

> They put poison in my food
> and when I was thirsty they gave me vinegar to drink.

Neither of these substances would have been pleasant to taste, or useful to drink, and in the context of Psalm 69, it is the work of enemies to offer such bitter things.

Mark has two references in his passion narrative to this incident. The first is at the beginning (Mark 15.22, 23): 'They brought Jesus to the place called Golgotha, which means "Place of a Skull", and they offered him drugged wine, but he did not take it.' There was nothing ominous or bitter about that. The drugged wine would have been offered as a painkiller, but Jesus did not take it. Jesus was not intending to reduce the suffering which he knew was his destiny. He was the suffering servant, and he stood in the tradition of Isaiah's suffering servant. Towards the end of the time on the cross, Mark describes a repetition of the offer, but this time it was not the soldier, but 'someone' who 'ran and soaked a sponge in sour wine and held it to his lips on the end of a stick' (Mark 15.36). On both occasions the drink was of a medicinal nature, and on neither occasion was there any indication that Jesus drank it.

Matthew also has two references to a drink at the cross. The first is at the beginning of the crucifixion (Matthew 27.34). Jesus is given 'a drink of wine mixed with gall to drink'. Matthew suggests that Jesus is offered something offensive and bitter, which was all part of the hatred inflicted on Jesus in his crucifixion. Then at the end of the crucifixion, Matthew has the same as Mark, 'One of them ran at once and fetched a sponge, which he soaked in sour wine and held up to his lips on the end of a stick' (Matthew 27.48).

Luke has no reference to drink at the outset of the crucifixion. He replaces the incident with Jesus talking to the women of Jerusalem. At the end of the crucifixion, Luke describes the giving of the drink in terms of mockery by the soldiers. 'The soldiers joined in the mockery and came forward offering him sour wine' (Luke 23.36). There is no reference as to whether Jesus accepted it, or consciously rejected it, but the feeling is that the soldiers probably held it near his lips, and then pulled it away teasing him.

John, like Luke, has only the one reference to the drink: 'A jar stood there full of sour wine; so they soaked a sponge with the wine, fixed it on hyssop, and held it up to his lips' (John 19.29). Jesus then received the wine. John's account is very much a fulfilment of the verse in Psalm 69.21. Jesus completes the unfinished business of the old covenant by his victory on the cross.

17

ON THE GIVING UP OF THE SPIRIT

Kind Father, Lord, my Saviour,
your head bowed,
your spirit passed across,
I appeal to you with all my strength
that you stoop, full of mercy,
and receive my spirit at the very end,
into the hands of the Father,
to breathe your last for me,
and to hold me up.
My living prayer
is that you will raise me from the dead,
send back the flames as I come to you,
cause the darkness to flee,
let the evil spirits fall silent
and the principalities and powers shrink back.
Grant me that life which is full of your grace
by which I can swiftly come to you,
Lord Jesus Christ,
Amen.

I sleep, but my heart waketh.

(Song of Solomon 5.2)

Jesus died a true death, a real death. His spirit passed across. The very last act of Jesus' life was the giving up, or the handing over, of his spirit. It was the ultimate passive act. He let go of himself into the hands of God. All his life he had been reaching out to God, teaching about the Kingdom, calling on the Father, and now the final act of faith was his handing over of his own spirit.

The prayer also mentions that his head sunk, was bowed (John 19.30). This is following John's description. The other Gospels all say that he gave a loud cry, and then died. The bowing of the head is an act of humility. We bow our heads before the king, and so here the King who himself deserves honour is the one who bows his head to the Father.

The one who bows is also the one who can lift up the fallen and raise the dead, and is just the person to appeal to for help. This great crossing over of death, mysterious, bewildering, in some senses unknown, is so fully dealt with in the Gospels and the Epistles. There is no need to fear. Christ is raised, and is the first-fruit of those who will rise from the dead. Yet the thrust of the discussion about resurrection is not so much of it happening at death. Far more important is that it will happen in God's time, and it will be for a much bigger group of people. Here in the prayer, the great end has been narrowed down to our own end, a personal confrontation between us and God, and the personal fear of the hour of death: flames, darkness, evil, principalities and powers.

The whole tenor of these prayers is the turning of the events of the death of Jesus into a personal source of salvation. They are, in that sense, private prayers. They are a making personal, the universal act. That is often how it is received and understood, and that is also how the gospel picture of Jesus is portrayed. He is the one who saw the individual's need, and he spoke directly to named people. He was there for him or her, and now through the humility of his death, the handing over of his spirit to God, he is available to all of us, individually, and is the one who will welcome us through death, into life.

18

ON THE CLOSED EYES

Omnipotent, eternal God,
light of light and source of all our seeing,
who by your holy death
have closed the eyes
by which you saw the heavenly secrets,
and the glorious face of your exalted Father.
I give you thanks and plead with all piety,
that in whatever way my soul suffers
by its own light,
you will grant me forgiveness
by the honour of your holy sight,
Lord Jesus Christ,
Amen.

Behold, thou art fair, my love; behold, thou art fair; thou
hast doves' eyes.

(Song of Solomon 1.15)

Seeing, so intimately linked with understanding in the contem-
plative tradition, is an aspect of Jesus' life which gave him
insights into the heavenly secrets. He wanted to open people's
eyes to the secrets of the Kingdom of God, and through his love
of people his ministry was also to the blind, giving them back
their sight. Eyes are the windows through which the outer,
material world meets the inner world of the spirit.

For the blind there are other routes. The spirit is not limited
to sight, because the heart is not limited to sight. It is far more
important to love God and our neighbour than to have a keen
eye. In fact, the power of sight can be misused. We can sin with
our eyes as easily as with anything else: 'And if your eye causes
your downfall, tear it out; it is better to enter into the kingdom
of God with one eye than to keep both eyes and be thrown into
hell' (Mark 9.47).

Yet sight has a mysterious power, tied up as it is with light, and
light is so much part of God's life. It was his first act of creation
on the first day, and the eye, and indeed the whole world,
depends on the existence of light to function.

What heavenly secrets did Jesus see, and what was the face
of his exalted Father like? Jesus' descriptions were rarely just
visual. He described processes by which the usual worldly

standards and protocol are radically changed. The poor are in front of the rich, the humble precede the powerful, the unwanted find a loving Father, and the sad are given reason to rejoice. So it is not with a cool artist's eye that Jesus sees. He sees in the dimension of love.

The face of his Father is another matter. For centuries the Jews had rejected the making of any representation of God. It was the first commandment of the great Mosaic law: 'You must not make a carved image for yourself, nor the likeness of anything in the heavens above, or on the earth below, or in the waters under the earth' (Exodus 20.4). It was not in Jesus' tradition to picture God, but more broadly he would sense him as closely as a human father, the protection, security, wisdom, the power and the strength. These are qualities that do not have their features depicted in art, but in law, and in human behaviour. In his death, Jesus became God's loving work of art most accurately portrayed. He is the true icon, through whom we see God, and by whom the heavenly secrets are revealed.

19

ON THE NOSTRILS

O most merciful Father,
I thank you
that you were filled
with the sweetest scent of all the virtues,
and at the very end of your life,
which we venerate,
sealed your nostrils
and handed over your spirit.
Grant that whatever my nostrils
have breathed in
of the stench of sin
you may expel from me,
worthless that I am,
Lord Jesus Christ,
Amen.

I have come into my garden, my sister, my spouse: I have gathered myrrh with my spice.

(Song of Solomon 5.1)

The beauty of fragrant scent and the stench of polluted air; the freshness of a dawn breeze and the putrid smell of rotting flesh: the world contains the whole range. It is a continual struggle to stem the tide of pollution. It is a major concern for people at the end of the twentieth century. We see little way out of the mess, except on a personal level trying to be more thoughtful about waste, exhaust emissions, overcrowding and disease. It is easy to get dispirited, since on the world level so little seems to be done, so little sense of a one-world responsibility for the health of the planet. Greed, selfishness, self-preservation at all costs are the motives that lie behind pollution, and of course they are, in the end, self defeating.

God created a world with all its beauty and integrated life intact. Humanity was made in the image of God, reflecting God's beauty and given a divine purpose. Humans were made to fit into the world and to be pleasant, and to be pleased by the world. It was never meant to be a titanic struggle. We were given senses to appreciate the beauty of it and to make use of it, but humanity lost its way. We hardly know now what it is we could be like, or what we should be like. We have gone so far away from the original intention of what it is to be human.

We have, though, one example in whom the sweet savour of

the virtues can be experienced. Goodness has its own scent, and Christ Jesus walked in the sweet-smelling scent of holiness. He sweated blood. He was fully human and needed his feet washed like any other human being; 'he shared man's smell', let's not get too precious about it. He showed us what it would be like to be fully human, and yet sanctity has its own odour, and it is anything but the odour of death.

Jesus was anointed with sweet-smelling ointment (Matthew 26.7f; Mark 14.3f; Luke 7.37f; John 12.3f). He let himself be loved and cared for by people, and by women whom many others considered disagreeable, but that was his task, his vision, his purpose and his joy. He transformed inhumanity, the stench of sinful nature, into a sacrifice good and acceptable to God.

The one praying here asks Jesus to cast out 'whatever (these) nostrils have breathed in of the stench of sin', so that they may be transformed, purged, into a sweet-smelling sacrifice acceptable to God. 'Live in love as Christ loved you and gave himself up on your behalf, an offering and sacrifice whose fragrance is pleasing to God' (Ephesians 5.2).

20

ON THE EARS

O God, my Lord,
who,
in the moment of death,
was deaf to my wretchedness
but with ears open to the inward will
of your Father's way.
I give you thanks,
and in so doing,
I ask forgiveness for these ears
whose hearing has been polluted
by the evil things that they have heard.
I pray
that never might I have to hear
in the day that will come,
the judge's sentence
equal to the faults that I have heaped up,
and that the fire of judgement
may not separate me eternally
from the fire of your love,
Lord Jesus Christ,
Amen.

O my dove, that art in the clefts of the rock, in the secret places of the stairs, let me see thy countenance, let me hear thy voice.

(Song of Solomon 2.14)

Hearing is one of the most powerful of the senses. The ears are the means by which we hear; and what complicated, sophisticated pieces of apparatus they are: inner, middle and outer, and two of them balanced, like the eyes and the hands and the feet. The prayer, though, is not concerned with the biology of the ear, but with its moral function, with what it allows itself to hear. In some ways we could say the ear cannot help hearing. That leads us on to the person whose ear it is, and the way in which that person regulates the activity of hearing: what they desire to hear, or to avoid hearing. That in turn leads on to the circumstances of the life which creates the sounds and regulates the opportunities to choose what you hear. If you live in a busy city, on a main road, beneath the flight path of jet aeroplanes, then however much you want to live in peace, the will is restricted.

The senses and the will are brought together, and their relation and interaction are what make up the essence of the prayer. With enormous gratitude from the writer, Christ was deaf to his wretchedness. At the point of death, Christ turned a deaf ear to those things which would bring judgement onto the one praying: such willed deafness was an act of forgiving love, typical of Christ as he died on the cross for others. So the ear has two functions, one to be deaf to past sins, the other to be acutely open to the inward will of the Father's way, or voice.

How can the hearing be polluted? Not surely by hearing things we can't help but hear, such as news of tragedy and disaster, and the general traffic of the world's noise, no: but by consciously seeking out to hear of other people's misfortune in order to gloat, or to search out the record of one's own praise, or to tune into the voice of evil for the immediate pleasure it brings, or with one's inward ear to be led astray into fantasies far removed from the reality of God's purpose.

The final part of the prayer concerns the voice of the judge in judgement, and of hearing the sentence of the Heavenly Judge. The image of the courtroom is still very resonant for those who have anything to do with the law and the courts of today. The words of the convicted are listened to acutely, the words of the witnesses the same, and the final word of the judge is waited for with expectancy. This prayer is a plea not to hear a sentence which is justly deserved, but to appeal to the love and mercy of the Heavenly Judge: so that the fire of judgement may not be separated from the fire of God's love, and the voice we hear may be sweet.

21

ON THE SIDE OF CHRIST

O Dispenser
of the medicine of salvation
who let the lance pierce
and open your side:
open to me I beg
as I knock at the door of life,
and once inside,
I will confess that it was I who wounded you
with the wounds of my sins.
This I will do
by the healing medicine of your mercy,
that I may never be held guilty
of receiving your body and blood
except my soul be filled to the brim
with your love.
You,
who are the price paid for me,
may you also be the prize,
Lord Jesus Christ,
Amen.

My beloved put his hand by the hole of the door, and my bowels were moved for him.

(Song of Solomon 5.4)

Ever since St John recorded the incident where a Roman soldier pierced the side of Christ and blood and water flowed out (John 19.34), there has been speculation about its significance. St John is at pains to stress its veracity: 'This is vouched for by an eyewitness, whose evidence is to be trusted. He knows that he speaks the truth, so that you too may believe . . . [a] text says "They shall look on him whom they pierced"' (John 19.35–37, quoting Zechariah 12.10).

The two particular interests of the writer of this prayer are the eucharist as the medicine of salvation, and the actual sense of entry into the body of Christ. St Paul often wrote about being 'in Christ', and here in St John is a door that will allow that entry. The sacramental significance of blood in the eucharist, and water in baptism, is also an important theme in this prayer: his blood is not only drink to nourish, but medicine to purge. Yet the imagination is taken much further as the wound opens up a way into the heart of Christ. Augustine describes the wound as an open door, like the door into the Ark through which the family of Noah, and the animals, went in safety. The wound which the lance inflicted in Christ has become the door, which once we are through, then there is the time of confession and the hope of forgiveness.

George Herbert's poem 'The Bag' describes it like this:

If ye have anything to send or write
I have no bag, but here is room:
Unto my Father's hands and sight
Believe me, it shall safely come.
. . .
Look, you may put it very near my heart.

Christ's heart is the post-box and the messenger by which our prayers can be delivered to God. Indeed our prayer is the very spear which pierces the side of Christ: Herbert's 'Christ-side-piercing-spear', from his poem 'Prayer'. The arrow in the heart is the symbol of love. St Theresa of Avila felt it as a reality in her devotion to the Lord. Christ's heart was full of love for the world, and in the crucifixion his heart was pierced. Only love can survive the up and down struggles of human life. Only a true self-giving love can allow the failures and the pains to be redeemed and to set things back in motion.

With our pleas driven into the heart of Christ, we find 'the healing medicine of his mercy'. The final lines of the prayer are very packed. The first image is from 1 Corinthians 11.27 where we are bidden not to eat or drink unworthily at the eucharist. The second image is of the servant taking on the sufferings of the master; and the third image is of Jesus, who paid the price of our ransom, being also our prize at the end, the prize for our suffering with him.

22

ON THE SEPULCHRE

Lord God,
you are the glory of the faithful
and the life of the just,
you restore what has been broken,
and once restored, preserve
what neither heaven, nor earth, nor sea
could take hold of.
You willed to be placed
in a single narrow sepulchre.
I give you thanks
and through the honour of your sacred body
which rested in the grave
without the wasting of corruption,
I beg you to allow me
such a seat of quietness
the rest of perfect bliss,
and a place of coolness, light and peace.
Lord Jesus Christ,
Amen.

My beloved is gone down into his garden, to the beds of spices.

(Song of Solomon 6.2)

There is a great peace which descends on the account of the passion at this stage. Indeed, the passion is over, it is spent. One tradition has Jesus now descending into hell to rescue souls, but for the moment we are invited to be with the body in repose. They gently lay him down in Joseph's unused tomb, surrounded by the green of the garden. The dissipated interest of the crowd, the evening light and muffled sounds, the sabbath quietly drawing its blanket over the world, the closing of the eyelids, these are the only things we can surmise.

After the clanging, noisy and painful passion, here is the quiet of the day, paradise, the 'quietis'. Believing in the after-life we can have confidence in this pacific state, that will give rest to all the turmoil of the world's pains, diseases and discontents. The tomb is a seed-bed of hope. From it Christ rose, and emerged victorious and full of glory with renewed power to bring salvation and rescue to a flailing world.

The unique creative act of resurrection was managed in the silence and solitude of the sepulchre. Jacob Epstein's great sculpture of the Raising of Lazarus is a most powerful image of the risen Christ, and this unbandaging, which shifted the whole fulcrum of the world by its energy, was the act in the sepulchre, and the sepulchre was cool, light and peaceful.

Out of the heat of the battle on Calvary, in the time of rest on the sabbath, new things were growing, new shoots rising, new life emerging. The tomb is the womb of the resurrection. This is such a mystery, we will never know for certain what exactly happened. The disciples were there and they described their experience in such a homely way, with none of the apparatus of deceit. We rest our case in silence.

23

INTO HELL

Lord God,
sower of the seed of hope, advocate of good counsel,
defender of the law, judge of the erring,
restorer of the suffering;
for our sake you deigned to descend into hell,
so that you could return the living spoils
to the place above.
I thank you,
Lord Jesus Christ,
and I adjure you, O most High,
to grant me, the most unworthy of all,
never after my death to push back my spirit
into the power of hell.
You,
who liberated all those imprisoned
in the ghastly hole of hell,
did not take fright at frightful things,
but descended and conquered.
The gates of hell did not prevail against you,
but you broke their hinges
with the authority of one who overpowers,

and having freed the captives
you brought them the spoils of salvation,
Lord Jesus Christ,
Amen.

Set me as a seal upon thine heart, as a seal upon thine
arm: for love is strong as death; jealousy is cruel as the
grave.

(Song of Solomon 8.6)

'He descended into hell' is both a terrifying and a comforting
notion; terrifying because the picture of hell we have is everything that is most awful, cruel, painful and unbearable. This
prayer makes it a place of imprisonment, with gates suitably
massive, everyone's nightmare castle with dungeons. In the
ancient three-tiered universe, it is the place beneath. Jesus
descended into it before he rose from it and ascended from
there into heaven.

Yet it is also comforting because the prayer is a picture of the
castle being stormed and of the spoils. The spoils are the un-
redeemed souls, being brought out through the doors now
off their hinges: 'In the spirit also he went and made his
proclamation to the imprisoned spirits, those who had refused
to obey in the past' (1 Peter 3.19–20).

Christ's suffering for our sins gave him the authority and the
power to do this. As the souls and bodies of the doomed are

70

locked in bodily pain and suffering, Jesus descends to bring them into his own spiritual state: 'That was why the gospel was preached even to the dead: in order that, although in the body they were condemned to die as everyone dies, yet in the spirit they might live as God lives' (1 Peter 4.6). As before, the writer of the prayer makes this myth his own. He asks Jesus to guard him from the possibility of falling back into the state of hell.

We have some modern hells by which to judge the reality of this prayer. We have the concentration camps of the Second World War to contemplate. They are so close to us historically, and we may say where was God, or his son Jesus, in that? Where was the rescuer tearing down the gates? Two answers come to my mind, one very unsatisfactory: the political will to defeat Nazism involved this country and many others in war. It was tragically too late to affect the fate of 6 million Jews, but not to halt, in the end, the victory of a diabolical philosophy that lay behind the holocaust.

The second answer to 'where was God in the concentration camps?' can only really be stated by those who suffered, but would it be true to say that God was himself being killed each time one of his children was being killed? There is an air of the fanciful about this answer. The physical suffering, humiliation, demoralization is impossible for us to contemplate. Death might have come as relief, in some deeply tragic sense. Our faith has at its centre a tortured God, a crucified God, a humiliated God. We can say, perhaps inadequately to those who have really suffered, our God has known the worst that humankind can do.

24

THE RESURRECTION

O life of the one who is dying,
health of the one who is sick,
and last remaining hope of the deserted!
You are the resurrection of the dead,
who on the third day
rose again for the lost in hell below
the chains of death
smashed about you,
free and full of joy.
I thank you,
most high God,
and ask you for this
in my wretched state;
a share in the first resurrection
through the forgiveness of my sins,
and a place in the second resurrection
with all the saints,
without an end,
Lord Jesus Christ,
Amen.

Many waters cannot quench love, neither can the floods drown it: if a man would give all the substance of his house for love, it would utterly be contemned.

(Song of Solomon 8.7)

The resurrection is the cause of enormous joy, because it upturns so many of the things that bring us down: death, sickness, doubt and, in this prayer, everything that has to do with hell. Jesus, responding to the will and desire of God to make all things new, sets the resurrection in motion. First, through God he generates his own, and through his own, those whose love and desire is to be with God. That is cause for great thanksgiving.

The act of being raised up, the moment when God's will and Jesus' obedience coalesced, when heaven touched earth and in the realm of time eternity was made real, that unimaginable moment which is veiled in silence and hiddenness, is described here in the act of releasing the chains of death. They are smashed with the superhuman strength of God's power, and that release brings such joy. Christ having defeated death himself, sets about releasing those enchained in hell.

'He descended into hell.' Jesus' victory on the cross was not a matter of personal and private satisfaction. It was an act wholly for others, and the first act of his victorious state was to descend in love among those who needed him most. Christ first descends to bring the dead to life with him. The leaping Christ of the resurrection is a wonderful picture of this drawing people

73

by the hand over the abyss of darkness and death into safety, light and peace.

The prayer is a cry for each one of us to be sharers in the benefits of this resurrection, and there are two resurrections spoken of, which reflect the ideas of Revelation 20.4–6. This is a highly imaginative and rather complicated scene mixed up with the thousand-year period, or millennium, of testing. The martyrs who have remained faithful in their witness to Jesus come to life again and reign for a thousand years: 'Blessed and holy are those who share in this first resurrection! Over them the second death has no power; but they shall be priests of God and of Christ, and shall reign with him for the thousand years' (Revelation 20.6).

The second resurrection is the way to life of all who have been faithful and whose names are written in the book of life. The prayer has a simpler version of this, in which we can ask God for salvation, first from our sins, and then to join him, in his own time, at the second resurrection with all the saints. These are the holy men, women and children whose love of God has brought them to the fulfilment of their desire.

25

AGAIN ON THE RESURRECTION

Omnipotent and sempiternal God,
consolation of the sad,
strength of those who labour,
yours is a unique and singular mercy.
You appeared first
after the glorious resurrection
to Mary Magdalen coming from the tomb,
whom naming, you consoled,
that the sin of the human race
might be cast out from its source.
I thank you
and call on your inexhaustible kindness
to lift me up,
praying,
if I may and unworthy as I am,
to discover confidence and consolation,
in the face of your divine majesty,
Lord Jesus Christ,
Amen.

My beloved spake, and said unto me, Rise up, my love, my fair one, and come away. For, lo, the winter is past, the rain is over and gone.

(Song of Solomon 2.10–11)

The heart of this prayer is the resurrection appearance of Christ to Mary Magdalene. It was Jesus' first appearance, and it was to a woman. The echo back to the appearance of the Lord God to Eve in the garden has always been strong in Christian tradition at this point, and the shape of redemption makes it a happy coincidence, although coincidence is perhaps too light a word for the purposes of God.

'Whom naming, you consoled': how succinctly that is put, as it is in St John's Gospel, spare in word and action but full of emotion and hidden echoes. The Lord God named the creatures at the beginning because he knew them for what they were, and now Jesus, who knew Mary Magdalene, names her, and her desperate search for the one she loved and had lost comes to rest in the hearing of her name in the familiar tone, and from the beloved voice.

There is no escaping, in theological tradition, the connection between the sin that Eve's disobedience brought to the world and the redemption worked through the death of Christ. So it was to a woman first that the reality of that redemption came. Such was the thinking of St John the Evangelist.

What of us? We call on the omnipotent and sempiternal, or

everlasting, God to comfort us with the calling of our name, to lift us up in our grief for our failures and sin, and to discover confidence and consolation in his majestic countenance.

The human is also the divine as seen in the face of Christ. The resurrection has brought the two together most vividly. Now we see what it is all about. It is clear in the face, and deeper even in the countenance, or look. The look has an intention behind it, the face can be vacant, but the look from which we so often shy, because of our sense of failure, is the look of love, so vividly expressed in Herbert's poem 'Love':

> Ah my deare
> I cannot look on thee.
> Love took my hand, and smiling did reply,
> Who made the eyes but I?

And the look is the look of complete knowledge and forgiveness from the Creator, the Father, the Lord.

References and Further Reading

The text of the Latin prayers is to be found in 'An Ancient Manuscript of the Eighth or Ninth Century, formerly belonging to St Mary's Abbey, or Nunnaminster, Winchester', ed. Walter de Gray Birch F.S.A. (London and Winchester, 1889). The numbering of the prayers in that book and this are different. For those wishing to research the prayers, the numbers correspond in the following way: my number 1 is Birch's number 16, my number 2 is Birch's number 17, and so on.

Other useful books for further reading are:

Bradley, S. A. J. (tr. and ed.) (1982) *Anglo-Saxon Poetry*, Everyman.

Brown, M. P. (1996) *The Book of Cerne*, The British Library and University of Toronto Press.

Campbell, J. (ed.) (1991) *The Anglo-Saxons*, Penguin Books.

Mursell, G. (comp.) (1997) *The Wisdom of the Anglo Saxons*, Lion.

Raw, B. (1990) *Anglo-Saxon Crucifixion Iconography and the Art of the Monastic Revival*, Cambridge University Press.

Symons, T. (ed.) (1953) *Regularis Concordia*, Thomas Nelson.